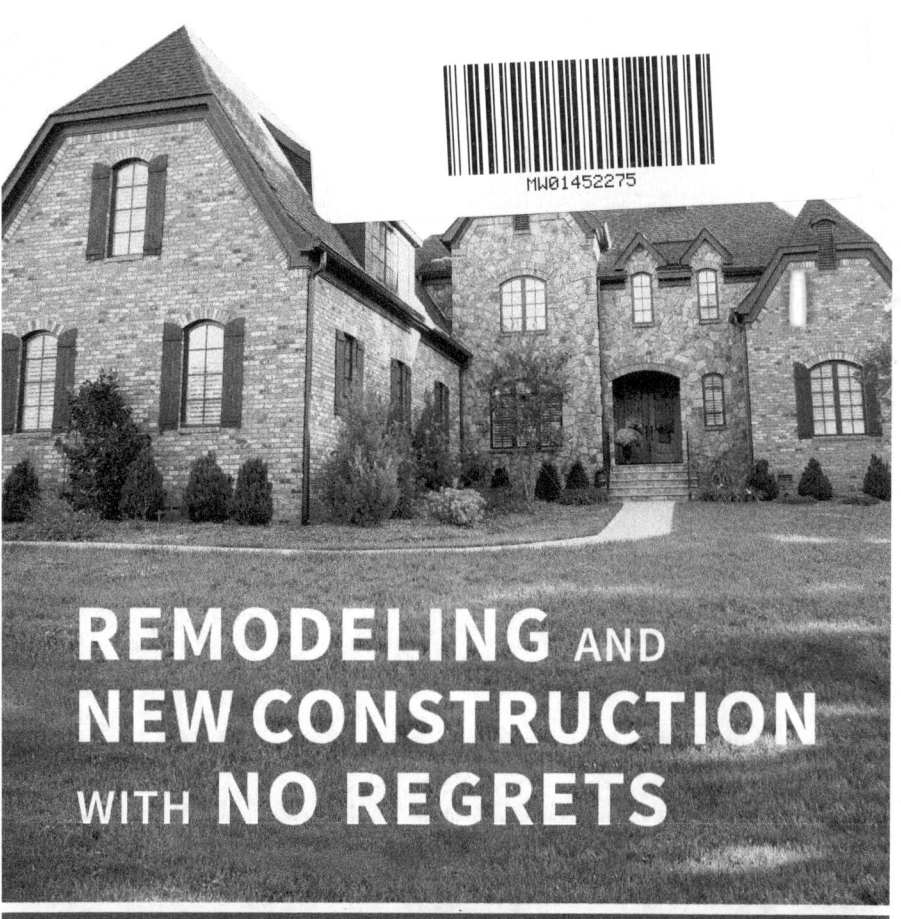

REMODELING AND NEW CONSTRUCTION WITH NO REGRETS

How to Avoid the Most Common and Frustrating Mistakes Homeowners Make

By Gary R. and Pam A. Palmer
with Trish Stukbauer

outskirts
press

REMODELING and NEW CONSTRUCTION with NO REGRETS
How to Avoid the Most Common and Frustrating Mistakes Homeowners Make
All Rights Reserved.
Copyright © 2020 Gary R. and Pam A. Palmer with Trish Stukbauer
v5.0

PalmerCustomBuilders.com
Palmer Custom Builders®

The opinions expressed in this manuscript are solely the opinions of the authors and do not represent the opinions or thoughts of the publisher. The authors have represented and warranted full ownership and/or legal right to publish all the materials in this book.

This book may not be reproduced, transmitted, or stored in whole or in part by any means, including graphic, electronic, or mechanical without the express written consent of the publisher except in the case of brief quotations embodied in critical articles and reviews.

Outskirts Press, Inc.
http://www.outskirtspress.com

ISBN: 978-1-9772-1501-7

Cover Image by Gwendolyn Belle Design
Front Photo by Gary R. Palmer
Back Photo by Kori Hoffman

Outskirts Press and the "OP" logo are trademarks belonging to Outskirts Press, Inc.

PRINTED IN THE UNITED STATES OF AMERICA

Disclaimer

This book is meant for informational purposes only and is not intended to be construed as financial, tax, legal, real estate, insurance, or investment advice. We always encourage you to reach out to a qualified professional in your specific area of the country for specifics regarding your personal situation.

Table of Contents

Dedication i
Acknowledgments iii
Introduction v
1. Should We Stay or Should We Go? 1
2. Is the Sky Really the Limit? 8
3. Can We Really Do This? 13
4. Don't Go Your Own Way 18
5. Who Should You Trust? 23
6. Now, Who Do We *Really* Trust? 31
7. Money Matters 37
8. Listen Up! 46
9. The Devil Really Is in the Details 51
10. Are You Going Through a Phase? 59
11. Are We There Yet? 65
12. Expect the Unexpected 70

About The Authors 75

Dedication

This book is dedicated to all homeowners who are contemplating remodeling, adding a new addition, renovating, or building a custom home, from a Licensed and Professional Contractor who is passionate about our business and about bringing our clients' dreams to life!

Acknowledgments

Thank you to all the clients who have entrusted us with their homes throughout the years. We appreciate our business associates - Communications: Trish Stukbauer; Our IT Team: Paul & Ray; Digital Marketing Team: Rachel, Ryan, Tim, Gwen & Derek; and Business Consultant: Michael Stone. We also value our long-term relationships with employees, tradespeople and vendors whose excellence reflects our commitment to meet or exceed client expectations - time after time. And finally, a very special thanks to our families, friends, and of course, God.

Introduction

Regrets. We've all had a few. Opportunities we missed. Doors we opened that perhaps were better left closed. Chances we didn't take because the outcome was just too uncertain. While regrets are, unfortunately, all too common in our day-to-day lives, one aspect of your life in which you don't want to have any regrets is in your next remodeling project or your new custom-built home. Why? Because, when it comes to an endeavor that can be one of the largest single investments many people will make, regrets are far too costly. That's true both in terms of the financial impact poor decisions can have and the intangible costs of living with a poor choice for years to come.

As qualified professional contractors with more than three decades of experience in all facets of home remodeling, additions, home renovations and repairs, and new custom home construction, we've heard from countless satisfied customers who have done things the correct way. Sadly, we've also had other folks come to us to correct the things that their previous builder, contractor or handyman didn't do, did incorrectly, or simply shouldn't have done in the first place. Over the years, we've listened to and learned from both the wonderful experiences and the poor ones and used them to establish our own solid processes.

While those processes ensure that our own clients are well taken care of, we wanted to do more. After all, we can't help everyone in person – as much as we would *like* to – so we took the time to assemble this book. In the following pages you'll find the biggest mistakes we've seen homeowners make over the years – from hiring the wrong firm to not planning for the home they *need*, to fundamental financial miscalculations that can sabotage a project. It is our hope that you will learn from these experiences and use them to systematically eliminate the chance of regrets cropping up in your project.

But before we talk about the largely external issues that can influence your project, we feel that it's only fair we open with a dirty little secret that few professional contractors are eager or even willing to address with potential clients. It's almost universally true that no matter how honed our skills, how extensive our training, how broad our education, or how substantial our expertise, one of the most important pieces of your home remodeling, home renovation or new home construction project is simply beyond our control - because that vital piece is you! If you begin your project with the right attitude, the correct perspective and with an open mind, you stand a much better chance of being satisfied with your results and having no regrets. But just what *is* the right approach?

Attitude Is Everything!

As true professionals, there is nothing we want more than happy clients, and we thoroughly believe your happiness is tied to how ready and willing you are to tackle a project, how cheerfully your family can accept some necessary "inconveniences" that ultimately lead to a greater good, and how much personal responsibility you are willing to take as a true partner in your project.

We feel that the best projects come about when clients are engaged partners. That doesn't mean getting mired in every mundane detail or trying to micromanage the process (which is a common and normal response to a prior bad experience), but it does mean playing a role in the overall scope of your project. This entails particulars such as establishing a realistic budget, instead of trying to piece your project together with low bids. It means making timely decisions, instead of delaying critical selections that can impact both the project timeline and your bottom line. It means deciding if now is the right time for your family to embark on this project and if you are willing to handle any challenges that may entail, such as temporarily living without access to one of your bathrooms or a kitchen, or even vacating your house entirely for a certain amount of time. Finally, it entails being realistic and committing to respectful, honest and open communication with the professional partners you hire.

Put It in Perspective!

It's a sad reflection of our times that respect for contractors may not be at the level it should be for experienced, Licensed Professional General Contractors. That's unfortunate, because qualified, professional general contractors bring a world of training and experience to the table.

This training far exceeds the bare necessity of just holding a business license, which only means that a company is legally permitted to conduct business – much like a florist, an advertising firm, a bookshop, or any other small business. While requirements vary by state, they generally far exceed the basics. To obtain a North Carolina General Contractors License, for example, an individual must prove their knowledge and competence by passing an exam and then demonstrate that they have the financial means to complete a project. There are three levels of licenses, each of which has specific working capital requirements. The highest, an Unlimited North Carolina General Contractor's License, allows a contractor to construct projects of unlimited value; an Intermediate license allows a contractor to construct projects up to $1,000,000, while a Limited license allows projects up to $500,000. Contractors who don't hold one of the higher licenses may not be able to complete your project if it exceeds their license limits.

Qualified contractors also rely on a network of highly educated and skilled professionals, ranging from the architects and structural engineers who work on your plans to the talented tradespeople who execute them. Just as an IT company bills you for installing and maintaining computer hardware, software and networks; your attorney bills you for a phone consultation; or your CPA charges to analyze your fiscal situation for tax advantages, these professionals should be paid for their time. Sadly, some homeowners approach a home remodeling project by trying to pay as little as they possibly can while still expecting professional-level results. These unrealistic expectations only lead to disappointment when the results of an unskilled worker's shoddy craftsmanship are revealed, and they may even lead to unfinished projects if a dishonest company opts to walk away midstream. Just as in other areas of life, you get what you pay for. If you want something of value – done by true professionals who understand your project and will care for your home as if it were their own – don't let the bottom line be your deciding factor.

Free Your Mind!

What's the final ingredient for a successful project? We believe that it's trust. You've done your homework. You've partnered with skilled professionals. You've been open and honest with them about your needs, your budget and your timeframe. Now, trust in their advice. Be open to creative suggestions they make based on their experience when they tell you that a product you want won't endure over time, or that the room layout you've envisioned might not best serve your needs. There may be an unexpected twist or turn during your project. There will be positive surprises, and there might even be a few kinks, so do your part by staying positive, realistic and understanding as the process evolves. If you have hired a true professional who has a solid process in place, not only will you not regret your decision; you will be more than pleased with the results.

CHAPTER 1

Should We Stay or Should We Go?

Regret #1: Moving When You Really Shouldn't

How to decide if remodeling your existing home is really "worth it."

It may have hit you when you were on a conference call, valiantly attempting to balance your laptop and business files on a cramped desk in the corner of the living room while trying - without much success - to muffle the rambunctious sounds of children playing in the background. Or perhaps the need for more space reared its ugly head as you were once again fighting the losing battle of cramming your groceries into the tiny closet that doubles as your pantry. Maybe your knees are screaming every time you walk up the stairs to your owner's suite. No matter what your point of frustration – a dedicated home office, a more functional kitchen, the lack of an accessible main level owner's suite, or something else – there comes a time in many homeowner's lives when the need for more, or more functional, space is clear.

When that need arises, many people automatically assume that they need to start over by moving to a larger home. While there are definitely times when it makes sense to move, bear in mind that moving can be far more disruptive than you think, cause a great deal of stress to your family, and cost much more than you envision. So how do you decide if remodeling or moving is right for you? We suggest you begin with an honest assessment of your family's situation, the limits and advantages of your existing home, and your current financial realities.

Your Family

One of the main determinants of whether or not you stay in your existing home should always be your family. Carefully consider the impact that a move would have on each of your family members. First, look at the very practical issues that impact your daily quality of life. Determine whether a move would require a change in your children's schools – and if that change would be positive or negative. Consider how a move would impact both your and your spouse's commute to work, church and any important or frequently attended activities. Look at property taxes and, if applicable, Homeowners' Association fees, in the neighborhood you're considering.

Don't neglect the importance of strong networks when weighing the pros and cons of a move. If the guys in the neighborhood get together for a much-loved poker game once a week, or the ladies enjoy their Wednesday afternoon socials by the pool, giving up a social structure that you are accustomed to can be stressful. Also think about the institutions that you frequent, such as your church, your gym, the bank you use and the accountant you trust. How would a move impact your ability to maintain these spiritual, social and business relationships?

Bear in mind that your family's ability to adapt to change will be different at different points in your life. If you are single or newly married and ready for your next adventure, a move may be an exciting option. If you have children in their early school years who have not yet established solid friendships or committed to extracurricular activities, moving now may be much easier and less demanding than attempting to move halfway through their junior year in high school. If you are nearing retirement, proximity to family and lifelong friends may play a key role both in your happiness and in planning for long-term support.

Likewise, consider your family's ability to handle a remodeling project **at this point in time**. If you always host a huge family get together for Thanksgiving, remodeling a kitchen in November is not a wise choice. When you are considering a remodeling project, the onus is on you to be open and honest with your contractor about major life issues, to get a realistic sense of the time required to complete your project, and to see how the two coincide. For example, you probably don't want to start building a swimming pool four weeks before your daughter's backyard wedding – unless you want the wedding pictures taken in a muddy, grassless construction zone. While temporary issues are not a reason to opt for buying a new home instead of remodeling, they can be a valid reason to postpone a project until the timing is better for your family.

One of the other things to keep in mind is that moving simply disrupts your family life. No matter how neat you are, there is a huge difference between keeping a clean home and keeping your home in "ready-to-show" condition for prospective buyers. "Ready-to-show" entails being vigilant about clutter, keeping personal items to a minimum, and possibly putting excess furniture, clothing, books, toys, sports accessories, lawn and garden equipment, tools, collectibles and more in storage until your home is sold.

Your Existing Home

Now is the time to take a brutally honest look at your neighborhood and your home's place in it. Do you love your neighborhood? Does it have the amenities that are important to you? Is it in the ideal location for your family? Could you purchase a home of similar or larger size with the amenities you need in the price range and area that you are looking for? In many areas of the country that may not be the case, as home prices have escalated quite substantially, and your home's resale value might not have caught up.

Next, consider your home. Do you love your home, but dislike one room or aspect of it? If you could just create more space, add a more functional kitchen or an extra bath, would you fall in love with your home all over again? If so, remodeling might be right for you. Don't worry if you can't envision exactly how the new kitchen, bathroom or addition can be added – after all, that's why you'll be hiring a professional. The key here is to decide if, with a few changes, the house that you are in now could be your dream home. Now is also the time to glance through any HOA documents or zoning requirements that will impact remodeling plans. While your contractor can sort through the minutiae, you do want to consider major issues, such as whether the type of addition you desire is permitted and what the setbacks on your lot will allow. A good professional contractor can do amazing things within the bounds of any applicable restrictions, but knowing what they have to contend with on the front end will ultimately save you time, money and potential heartbreak.

Finally, look at other homes in your neighborhood in relation to yours. If you are currently in the largest and most expensive residence, it might not make financial sense to invest more in it. Conversely, if your neighbors have recently updated their residences, you may need to invest in yours just to keep up. While we're definitely not advocating keeping up with the Joneses just for the sake of appearances, it is important to keep in mind that you are competing with your neighbors when it comes to your home's resale value. If the Parkers down the street updated their kitchen while yours is 10 years old, you will be at a competitive disadvantage when the time eventually comes to sell your home.

Financial Realities

That brings us to financial realities. It's crucial whether you are considering a move or a remodeling project that you understand the true cost of either one.

In Chapter 7, *Money Matters,* we'll take an in-depth look at how to finance your remodeling project. What you need to understand on the front end is that remodeling the correct way does cost money. The real world does not function like home improvement television shows. You can't **really** remodel a kitchen in 12 hours for $500. Why not? Because those shows usually use donated expertise, labor and products. They don't consider the weeks spent planning, ordering and retrieving materials; the time and funds spent to secure permits; or the actual price that real homeowners would pay for what they use. At this very early phase of your planning process, you don't need to get bogged down in details, but you do need to get a realistic idea of what remodeling projects that are similar to yours cost. Take the time to do some online research, to reach out to a local resource such as the National Association of the Remodeling Industry, and to talk with trusted friends who have gone through similar projects and with qualified professional remodelers. Bear in mind that while the intricacies of your project may be different, and the quality of materials that you select will impact your bottom line, this initial research is to get a realistic cost range to see if your finances are anywhere close to what you will need for what you want to accomplish. You can't for example, do a major upscale kitchen remodeling project, complete with new cabinets, appliances, flooring, lighting, fixtures and structural modifications for $22,500 - which is the average national cost of a minor kitchen facelift. But if you can afford to spend $22,500 and what you really want is closer to $80,000- $90,000, you might want to consider phasing in a project as your budget allows.

When most people weigh the costs of remodeling vs. moving, we find the vast majority will decide to remain in their homes, some may choose to delay remodeling until their finances are in line with what they envision, and in rare cases, some will decide to move into a home that's exactly what they are looking for. But before you opt to move for the sake of convenience, we always advise potential clients to consider the true cost of moving, which is likely much higher than you would anticipate. In fact, depending on which national study you look at, the real costs of moving can be anywhere from 10 percent up to 17 percent of your home's sales price. That number includes items like Realtor® commissions, necessary home repairs before selling, seller concessions, seller closing costs and moving costs. Added to that large percentage are the expenses for upfits and purchases for the new home, as well as possible increases in interest rates and property taxes.

It also doesn't include those annoying what-ifs of moving. For example, if you haven't already located or closed on your new home by the time yours sells, you'll need a temporary place to stay, which means that you'll have to move twice. Conversely, if you move before your existing home sells, you'll need to cover two mortgages for an undetermined period. Also, while you know the repair status of the elements in your existing home, you may be inheriting someone's problems when you move if there are issues that don't show up on your new home's inspection report. If the seller is making repairs, make certain they have been properly completed by a licensed, professional contractor - electrical, exterior wood, roofing, boxing, siding and subfloor structural issues often won't become apparent for several months or longer, when the cost to re-repair correctly will come out of your pocket.

Also remember when weighing the cost of remodeling vs. moving that with remodeling you are investing in your home. If planned and executed properly, you may recoup a large portion of your renovation expenses, particularly if you plan to stay in your home for a few more years. When considering the long-term monetary return as well as all the issues involved in deciding whether to remodel or move, it's vital to keep in mind what money can't buy. Your family's daily quality of life is far more important than a potential monetary return years down the road.

CHAPTER 2

Is the Sky Really the Limit?

Regret #2: Not Getting What Your Family Really Needs

*How to step away from "what you think is possible"
to consider what your family actually needs.*

When clients are in the initial stages of considering a home remodeling project or building a new custom home, we're often asked, "where and how do you even begin?" When we meet with potential clients, we often see them make two related mistakes that we want you to avoid - not knowing what they want and not knowing what they want to spend. Here's how to begin your project the right way, so you won't fall into either camp.

What You Want

First, if you're considering a home remodeling project, take the time to make a list of your concerns. Think simple statements such as: "I hate my kitchen; My master bathroom is ugly." Brevity is fine initially - just jot your thoughts down on paper.

Next, think about what isn't working for you now. These are the "pain points" that you will want your project to address. Don't fret about

IS THE SKY REALLY THE LIMIT?

how to design or construct your project at this stage, just think about what you would really like to change or add. A professional, experienced remodeler will know exactly how to achieve the end results you want and will guide you through the process. Examples of these "pain points" in a kitchen remodeling project can be anything from "I would love a kitchen that would allow me to feel connected to guests in the next room," to "I would love enough pantry space to get not just my food, but my pots and pans organized," or "I want a kitchen island." It could be as simple as "I hate my floor," or it could be as specific as "I want a Lava Stone countertop in glossy blue Azur with rounded edges and water grooves running into the sink." If it's important to you and your family, write it down and designate it as a priority.

When you complete these first steps, you will discover that you have defined the initial scope of your project, and that scope might be much greater or surprisingly less extensive than you first thought. (Bear in mind that your initial scope will change when you talk with a professional, qualified remodeler who can explain exactly what needs to be done – not just aesthetically, but structurally, functionally and schematically – to achieve your goals.)

In these initial stages, if there's something that you would like to include in your remodeling project if the sky were the limit, don't hesitate to write that down, too. Why? Because a professional remodeler may be able to surprise you. He might not be able to work that $4,500 designer-brand gas cooktop into your budget, but he might be able to show you a $1,500 model with many of the key features you mentioned that will come close to your dreams. But we'll discuss more about budget in a moment. What is important here is that you don't rule out a dream without considering the possibility. All too often, folks assume that something they want is unattainable and don't even ask – and that's a huge mistake when you're talking about a home that you will be living in day in and day out.

You follow much the same process when it comes to new home construction. Start by defining what you want in your family's home. Go through the same simple checklists by stating facts like: "We need a large master bedroom." "An open kitchen is important to us." What will emerge from this process is a list of items that you'd like to see in your new home. It will evolve into a practical guide that you can hand to a Design/Build Contractor that lists how many bedrooms and bathrooms you need, which living areas are important to you, and more.

Yet even more essential than determining what you need is understanding why you need it. For example, do you have a formal dining room on your wish list because you entertain formally often, or because it's what you expect to see in a custom home? Is there a luxurious soaking tub in your owners' suite because bubble baths are your favorite escape? Or do you actually prefer showers but have this costly option on your list because a Realtor once told you that soaking tubs were essential for resale value? We encourage clients not to get bogged in details - like picking out the down lights above your kitchen island - in this very initial stage, simply because plans evolve and those details will change. Yet at the same time, if there are aspects of your new home that are critically important to you, you'll want to at least note them now. Installing exotic hardwood floors throughout the main living areas carries a drastically different price point than installing basic carpeting, therefore, if it's essential to your happiness, that option should be factored into your initial equations.

Bear in mind that whether you are building new or remodeling to make your home feel like new, what your family wants and needs should be specific to you. Your list should reflect how you want to live – not what you've been settling for up until now. What you are hoping to create is a home design that fosters your family's ideal lifestyle – whether that's casual afternoon Monopoly games around a kitchen island or elegant evening gatherings centered around a pool house, quiet nights curled up with a book in your owner's suite, or video presentations to clients made from the comfort of your nicely equipped and properly sound-proofed home office. Design your home for the life you want your family to live – now and in the future.

What You Want to Spend

Next, give some concentrated thought to how much you really want to invest in your home. Since they don't do this every day, most homeowners don't have a solid grasp of what a remodeling project or a new custom-built home actually costs, but that's also okay at this point. Initially, your main concern should be with what you really want to invest in the home. Go ahead and start talking with your preferred bank to see what they say you can afford. Then, we recommend a far more personal "gut check" with you and your spouse to see what your finances will honestly support – which may be a very different number from what the bank tells you. Remember when you arrive at a number from the bank (or from yourself if you are considering financing your remodel out of pocket or with a home equity loan) that the number you are looking at is your *total* budget. That is far different from the cost of construction. Your total budget should include the cost of the lot for a custom home, or the cost of demolition and debris removal in a remodeling project. It should include the services of all the professionals you'll need throughout the course of your project – such as your contractor, architect, structural engineer, tradespeople and design consultants, the cost of governmental or HOA fees and permits, temporary utility hookups, and all of the costs normally associated with construction. You also need to build a contingency fund of as much as 10% to 15% of your project costs to cover anything that you decide to add or change later. It also protects you in case of emergences: If you run into anything unexpected behind the walls of your existing home or beneath the surface of your lot, you'll have the finances in place to cover it.

Now that you have an idea of what you *can* spend. You'll need to consider what you actually *want* to spend. How do you do that in a remodeling project? Consider your home's value and the market value of other homes in the surrounding area. Bear in mind that we are living in unprecedented real estate times. If a Realtor says your home is only worth $X per square foot today, look at the history of sales in your area and realize that values could escalate again in the future. Then consider intangibles such as how long you plan to stay in your home. Is it one year, five years, ten years, or are you never planning to move? The amount that you are willing to invest in a home you'll only be in for a year is probably markedly different than what you'd be willing to invest in your home if you plan on remaining in it for five years or even longer.

Going through this process will help you crystallize your thinking. Oftentimes, people considering a remodeling project may decide that they need a new home instead. That's okay, too, because they will have made a well-informed decision.

In either case, it's almost time to talk to a qualified, professional remodeler or custom builder who has substantial experience dealing with the type of projects you're considering. Being honest with your contractor about your hopes and budget is critical, because when you talk with this professional, you'll begin to officially define the project's scope and determine whether it is realistic within the confines of your budget. Don't lose heart if the initial proposal comes in over budget, because if you have clearly prioritized your needs, a qualified, professional remodeler may find practical ways to reduce costs or to phase in a remodeling project over time as your budget allows. Likewise, a talented architect can trim your project down to those essentials that are critical for your family. That's why we always recommend working with a Design/Build Contractor. Thanks to their work in the field, these professionals fully grasp what it costs to build the project they envision. This may save you substantial time and money (not to mention the heartbreak) that comes with designing a plan you want only to discover that it costs too much to build.

CHAPTER 3

Can We Really Do This?

Regret #3 Not Considering the Basics First

What you should investigate before you call a contractor.

It sounds simple enough: before you begin to build your new custom home or to embark on your dream home remodeling project that changes your home's footprint, make sure that you can accomplish what it is you are setting out to do. Yet when you're caught up in the excitement of beginning a project, the last thing that most people want to do is take what they view as an optional step that might further delay the process. We've talked about looking into finances and making certain that your family is emotionally prepared to begin a project. In this chapter, we'll look at the lot itself and why it's intelligent to take a few extra steps on the front end.

First, have a professional surveyor conduct a survey of your current property or the property you are considering buying for your new custom-built home. Many homeowners see this as an unnecessary expense for a remodeling project; after all, they reason, "I know where my property lines are, why should I pay someone to tell me what I already know?"

First, the odds are that you will need it. One of our remodeling clients, for example, opted not to have a survey done at closing when she purchased her residence, which she intended to remodel. Unfortunately for her, we had to have a current survey to obtain HOA approval for her remodeling project. That meant that she had to have the survey done anyway, which held up the renovation planning and approval process for an additional four weeks – an inconvenient and costly delay. Fortunately for her, the survey showed that there were no issues with her property. (We are finding on some projects now that the Building Permit, Zoning, FEMA or Water and Land Resources Departments may require a current property survey to issue a building permit or to perform an onsite property inspection at the conclusion of the project prior to issuing a final Certificate of Occupancy.)

Second, the survey might reveal something you didn't realize. Another client assumed they knew where their property line was and had an architect draw up an impressive two-car garage addition with a second-story owner's suite. When they came to us to build the project, we required that they have a physical survey done, since the side lot lines were very unclear. The survey revealed that they only had space for an oversized one-car garage, because they failed to properly plan for required side-lot setbacks. The architect had to redraw and reconfigure the garage footprint based on the new survey and buildable area. While this was a costly change, imagine what would have happened if the issue had not been discovered until after the addition was in process or completed! Depending on the circumstance, the client could have incurred tens of thousands of dollars in extra costs to rectify the situation and then start over. That's why we believe it's always wise to begin planning with a current survey in hand and the guidance of an experienced licensed General Contractor who can carefully lead you through the pre-planning and construction process.

Other homeowners have not been as lucky. When you don't do a survey or when you rely on one that was completed years ago (and thus doesn't take any property or zoning changes into account), you are running the risk of making some very expensive mistakes. According to The North Carolina Society of Surveyors, Inc., common issues revealed by surveys include encroachments across property lines or building restriction setbacks; issues with fences, walls and other landscaping features; placement of pool decks, the location of utilities and access ways; and the presence of flood zones. Imagine spending what could easily amount to tens of thousands of dollars on your dream landscape only to go through the trauma of having to tear it down and rebuild it because it's on your neighbor's property or it violates a setback or flood plain. The cost and inconvenience are only magnified once you begin to talk about a remodeling project that impacts not just your yard, but your home as well.

These traumatic situations can easily be avoided if you simply take the time to do things properly on the front end. Get a survey before you begin to plan your remodeling project if the project will change your existing home's footprint. If you are buying an existing home with the intent to remodel, plan on having a property survey done on the property. That way, you can order it far enough in advance that it won't cause any delays in the closing process. There's also a misconception that you don't need a survey because title insurance will "cover" you. In reality, "matters of survey" are only likely to be covered if a current survey is conducted **before** the title insurance policy is issued. While the NCSS does note that lender's policies may cover "matters of survey" without requiring a current survey, these policies typically only cover the lender in case of mortgage default and do not provide any protection for the homebuyer. Ultimately, taking the time to commission a current survey is by far the best insurance policy.

But what about new construction? The same caveats apply. If you are considering purchasing a lot – either before or as you begin to plan your home – a survey can tell you the same vital information about your building envelope and any restrictions of which you might not be aware.

There's always some confusion about which should come first – creating a home design or selecting the lot, and it's a bit of a "chicken and the egg" riddle. The best results naturally evolve when you look at both simultaneously, designing your home to take advantage of the distinctive characteristics of your home site. That way, your Design/Build Contractor and/or architect can be certain that windows are perfectly positioned to take advantage of your views or can camouflage any aspects of your lot – or your neighbor's home – that you don't want to see. In some cases, you may have your heart set on a particular plan, so you'll want to make certain that the lot you select allows for it – as far as the lay of the land, any property setbacks, building restrictions, and more. For example, if you know that you want a walkout basement, you'll have to select a lot with enough natural fall to accommodate it. If the lot you are considering will require a well and septic system, you'll want to be certain that it perks for the size of the home you want to build.

We talked about it briefly in the previous chapter, but now is also the time to make certain that what you want to build can be built in your neighborhood, taking any HOA restrictions, zoning issues, community architectural guidelines, or historic district guidelines into account. Key physical restrictions include things such as minimum or maximum square footage requirements, exterior material restrictions, the type and style of home that can be built there, the number of stories it may have, the type and size of secondary structures permitted on your property, and more. You'll also want to ask about any restrictions on the builder you can use. Some communities only permit certain builders to construct homes there. While that's fine if you want to use one of the builders on their list, it's not good if you have someone else in mind or if you don't "click" with one of their preferred builders.

You'll also want to consider the surrounding lots, who owns them, and what is likely to be or permitted to be built there. While you can't predict the future, asking a few questions of your Realtor and future neighbors can make a huge difference in your level of comfort with your new neighborhood. You'll also want to look at the existing Architectural Guidelines in a community, which may restrict the size, number of stories and architecture of a new custom-built home because it would simply look out of place.

CHAPTER **4**

Don't Go Your Own Way

Regret #4 Trying to Do It Themselves

*Why you should never try to play General Contractor
for your own project.*

It's only natural – and we might add, prudent – to try to stretch your budget in challenging economic times. When you are talking about basic home repairs, there are definitely things that you as a homeowner can do – depending on your skill level – and there are other things that are better left to professionals. However, when you expand the discussion from the basics of home improvement to tackling your own home remodeling project or building your new custom-built home, it's vitally important that you just say no to trying to tackle it on your own.

You might read that last paragraph with a raised eyebrow and think: "I'm handy. I can do this. I'm not an amateur like the people you see on those DIY gone wrong television shows. They're not talking about me!"

Rest assured; we are talking about you – and about everyone else who has ever tried to tackle an extensive home remodeling project or to build their own custom home. It's simply a bad idea to either try to build your own project or to play your own general contractor for a whole host of reasons that we'll only touch on here. What you need to remember is that the decision not to go it alone is **not** a reflection of your skill, desire, commitment or abilities. You may be an exceptional handyman, a talented woodworker or a gifted wall painter. If you are, there might be a place within the overall scope of your project where you can put your skills to good use, but we encourage you to work with your contractor to find that place if you so choose. The reality is that in a large-scale project, timing is critical, and professionals whose primary job responsibility is your project will get their work done much more quickly and efficiently than a homeowner who is balancing all of life's demands.

Okay, you reason, if I can't do it myself, surely, I can save money by cutting out the middleman, hiring the contractors and then managing them myself. While that sounds good in theory, the reality is that qualified professional contractors are just that – professionals – and there is much more to effectively managing a project than initially meets the eye.

First, as a homeowner, you are simply too close to your project - and you should be! After all, being passionate about your home remodeling project or new custom home is why you are embarking on this journey in the first place. However, when you delve into the day-to-day details of working with subcontractors, dealing with building inspectors, and keeping the neighbors happy, there are simply times when a more detached view is best. You need someone who can take a step back and look at the situation objectively. When you get frustrated, your general contractor should be there to assure you that a weather-related delay of one afternoon won't impact the overall timeframe. Conversely, they should be able to honestly tell you how ordering that hard-to-find granite color that you have your heart set on can delay the entire kitchen installation process by weeks. Having that rational third party looking out for the overall best interest of your project is essential.

Another main reason to hire a qualified, professional general contractor is that they have the training and experience to keep the big picture of your project in mind. This holds true for even the smallest details. Think of it this way: Imagine that after months of planning and construction – not to mention years of saving – you finally have the outdoor living area of your dreams. The pool you've always envisioned is set against a gracious seating area, the focal point of which is a massive stone fireplace – with an unsightly electrical junction box that you can see from every angle. It's all too often those jarring details that detract from the most carefully planned space. These missteps are most likely to occur on large-scale projects where tradespeople who don't usually work together may not be able to fully anticipate each other's needs.

For example, on one recent project, we built a pool house that included a family room, kitchen, full bathroom and laundry facilities, and also managed construction of the pool. While the pool company was responsible for building the pool, managing its construction gave us several advantages. First, we were able to ensure that the pool was sited at the correct elevation to flow with the rest of the construction and landscaping. Then, we could ensure that water, electrical and gas lines that were being run for the pool house were coordinated with those being used for the pool pumps and heater. Finally, understanding the big picture allowed us to better organize tradespeople to maximize efficiencies and reduce construction time.

Even less extensive projects can benefit greatly from coordination. For one project where we created an upstairs deck and screened porch, we coordinated the efforts of the stonemason to tie our staircase into a stone pathway leading to a raised terrace with a BBQ and sitting area. This ensured that the completed project flowed in a practical and aesthetically pleasing manner.

If you have a long-range plan for your remodeling project or new custom home that involves several phases, project management becomes even more vital. Having a contractor who understands your overall plan ensures that costly and time-consuming errors won't be made. For example, a stonemason laying a patio in Phase One won't cover a space where an electrical line will need to be buried in Phase Two.

But a general contractor is necessary for more than just coordination; they are essential in selecting the proper materials and team members from the very beginning. When it comes to selecting the materials that are perfect for your project, an experienced General Contractor has the vision and the resources to find exactly what you need and what will work in your application. They have many avenues for finding products, through a variety of vendors and other exclusive resources, not all of whom will deal directly with the public.

Even more important than the materials are the people who will use them. In a large-scale remodeling or new construction project, you will be working with more tradespeople than you can possibly imagine. To do the job correctly, you'll want to hire skilled, professional people who are experienced at what they do, do it well, and carry the proper licenses and insurance to protect your investment. You also want to be certain that you are getting a good value for your dollar. (Note that we specifically said value – not rock-bottom price, but we'll talk more about that in the next chapter!) While a typical homeowner might have a plumber they trust, or an electrician whom they are confident does good work, they are unlikely to know all of the trades they will need to complete their project: surveyors, architects and/or residential designers, structural engineers, demolition experts, lot clearers, heavy equipment operators, concrete companies, framers, masons, roofers, plumbers, electricians, HVAC contractors, sheet rock hangers, trim carpenters, painters, lighting designers, kitchen designers, cabinet makers, stucco installers, well drillers, septic system installers, irrigation installers, interior designers, landscapers, audio/visual installers, and more. Professional General Contractors spend years developing a design-build team (most of whom may never work directly with the general public) of responsible, loyal and accountable people to work on your project. This team undoubtedly adds value to the final product. Plus, their years of working together – and understanding each other's needs and habits – is mutually beneficial to everyone throughout the entire construction process.

In fact, no matter how good the tradespeople you hire are at their unique jobs, if you pull them in individually without having an experienced General Contractor diligently guarding the integrity of your project, the chances that something simple will be missed are high. By the time you notice what that is, it might be too late to correct the error. In even the best-case scenario in which the issue can be corrected, the duration of your project will be adversely impacted and as a result, project costs could rise. And your dreams are simply too important to let that happen! Just remember – an experienced General Contractor will add value to your project and give you peace of mind about your investment in your home.

CHAPTER 5

Who Should You Trust?

Regret #5 Not Hiring a True Professional

How to find a qualified, professional remodeling contractor or new home builder.

It's every homeowner's worst nightmare. Your dream kitchen renovation has begun. Your outdated cabinets and appliances have been removed, and the rock-bottom deal you got from your contractor has let you upgrade the new ones even more than you'd hoped. The discolored tile has been ripped out, plumbing pipes and electrical wiring are disconnected, and the exterior wall has been removed to make way for the expansion. You live with the mess through a long holiday weekend, looking forward to beginning reconstruction. Your contractor doesn't show up on Tuesday, but you're not alarmed, because you assume the rain delayed him. You are mildly panicked by Thursday, when your calls and emails have gone unreturned, but your heart sinks on Friday, when instead of his normally cheerful voice mail, you hear "the number you have dialed has been disconnected."

A contractor going out of business in the middle of your remodeling or new home construction project is the number one fear of most homeowners. An extensive remodeling project can be disruptive under even the best of circumstances, and a new construction project can take quite some time, yet what gets homeowners through both is picturing the end result. When a contractor folds mid-project, that end result is delayed exponentially. You have to find another contractor willing to jump into the chaos left behind. Your new contractor may be left with more questions than answers – not knowing what was done when, by whom, and how well, which causes further delays and costs as he or she tries to discover where and when to even begin. And that's if you can find a contractor willing to take on your job in the midst of likely legal proceedings against the previous company. All the while, your family will be living amid the debris of a job left undone.

One way to avoid all this is to heed the warning signs and do your research on the front end to ensure that you are selecting a qualified, professional remodeling contractor or new home builder. Here are a few things that we recommend you look into before you sign on the dotted line:

Make Sure the Company Is Licensed

If a company is not properly licensed to handle residential General Contracting work in your state, there's generally a reason. Bear in mind that in the vast majority of locations, a General Contractors license goes far and above holding a business license. A business license is just that – the credentials that are necessary to legally conduct any business. It's the same license that your local florist, copy shop or dry cleaner has to obtain to legally conduct business within the confines of your city, county or state.

In contrast, a General Contractor's license helps ensure that the contractor in question is knowledgeable in their field and understands the particular idiosyncrasies of building in your area. To obtain an N.C. General Contractors License, for example, an individual must prove their knowledge and competence by passing an extensive exam and then demonstrate that they have the financial means to complete a project. There are actually three levels of licenses, each of which has specific working capital requirements. The highest, an Unlimited North Carolina General Contractor's License, allows a contractor to construct projects of unlimited value; an Intermediate license allows a contractor to construct projects up to $1,000,000, while a Limited license allows projects of up to $500,000. Contractors who don't hold one of the higher licenses may not be able to complete your project if it exceeds their license limits. While license requirements vary from state to state, we offer North Carolina as an example of what you should be looking for when considering a contractor. Likewise, if your GC is not using licensed plumbers and electricians, the work these tradespeople are doing is suspect at best and, in the worst-case scenario, could even be hazardous.

Verify Their Credentials

Once you know that your contractor is properly licensed, the next step is to make certain that they are accredited members of their local or national Better Business Bureau, National Association of the Remodeling Industry, National Association of Homebuilders or other applicable trade organization. Why? Because membership in good standing in these critical watchdog groups indicates that your contractor is dedicated to excellence in their profession. It means that they are engaged and active members of the building community. While membership in and of itself does not guarantee competence, it goes a long way toward demonstrating that your contractor at least cares about what they are doing. By the same token, any unresolved complaints against your contractor filed with the Better Business Bureau should be a huge red flag that the company is not responsive to its customers.

Insurance Is a Necessity

Any reputable general contactor will carry insurance; it's not only an indication of their professionalism, it's a measure of the effort they will take to provide protection for you as the homeowner. Yet checking for insurance should extend beyond your GC to the contractors he or she hires. If the tradesmen hired by your contractor do not carry General Liability or Workers Compensation insurance, any mishap they or their employees suffer could become your very costly responsibility.

In the same vein, if a contractor is willing to work without pulling building permits or completing the proper inspections, or asks you to pull the permit, he's not doing so to save your time or money. It's typically because he is not qualified to pull the permit, or he knows that he is doing sub-par work that won't pass inspection. Here's why proper permitting pays off. In the first place, obtaining the necessary permits will ensure that your project is safe and up to code. Next, in this era of tighter mortgage requirements, more lenders are requiring code compliance checks before approving loans – which is something a permit ensures, whether you're looking to secure a renovation loan or to sell your house a few years down the road. If a residential construction project wasn't properly permitted and by state or county law it should have been, an insurance company may deny a homeowner's resulting future claim if the work wasn't constructed and inspected to meet residential building code requirements. It may also become an issue with the sale of a home.

Finally, and perhaps most importantly, permits give homeowners a level of confidence in the professionalism of their contractor. In fact, it's a definite red flag if a contractor asks you as a homeowner to pull a permit in your own name. That often means that the contractor is not properly licensed and thus is unable to pull the permit him or herself. Working with an unqualified contractor will cost you far more in the long run than the small fee that pulling a permit actually entails.

Even if they are doing good work - doing it without a permit ultimately can cost you your dream. Take one area family whose entire downstairs renovation was completed without a building permit. When they later failed to produce the necessary documentation, a building inspector required that they remove all the sheetrock (which had already been finished, trimmed out and painted), remove the cabinetry that was in place, and basically gut the entire area down to the studs to ensure that the proper insulation had been used. So not only did this family have to pay a fine for not getting a permit in the first place and then pay for a complex project twice, but they also had to endure the heartbreak of seeing their dream torn down and the emotional strain of rebuilding the project.

Completing work without a permit also may cost you when it comes time to sell your home. During the due diligence period of the sales process, most buyers will request a home inspection. If the home inspector discovers that work has been completed without securing a proper permit, he or she may recommend calling in a structural engineer, electrician or other tradesmen to determine if the work has been done to current Building Code standards. For example, if you finish your basement without a permit and the inspector questions anything, he may require that one of these professionals verifies the caliber of the work that has been done. As we mentioned earlier, that often entails removing sheetrock to verify that the structure, framing, electrical, plumbing, insulation, etc. all meet current code. In many cases, the required inspections will need to be completed by Building Code officials. These extra steps will cost you as the homeowner money – just to get the correct inspections in place - and may cost you even more if you have to take any corrective steps to replace sub-par work.

Even after the sale, you still may not be safe from the after effects of doing things improperly. If for example, a deck on your former home was not built properly or up to then-current code and an accident results from that poor construction, you could incur some liability for it. When all is said and done, getting the proper permits on the front end is a small price to pay for peace of mind.

Do They Have Experience?

One of the most important questions you should ask a potential contractor is how long they have been in business. Of course, everyone needs to start somewhere and even the finest general contractors in the country were once newbies, but should you let an inexperienced person learn the ropes and work out the kinks of their business on your project? Using an inexperienced person can prove costly in more ways than one – the extra time it takes as well as the money often required to fix things that weren't done correctly the first time. We personally think your project and your hard-earned money are better entrusted to someone who has some experience under their belts – and not just any experience. If the GC doesn't seem to have expertise in your particular type of project – whether it's construction or renovation, planning or project management – you should be very wary. Remodeling and new home construction are complex, long-term projects that require true experts to manage. Likewise, having a diversity of skills and widespread experience tends to make a contractor more capable of handling any unexpected challenges that may arise.

Reviews

These days, most people will do their due diligence by checking client testimonials on builders' and contractors' websites, reading Google reviews, scouring BBB listings, and looking at whatever neighborhood or local social media platforms are prevalent in your area. When reading these types of reviews, always consider the broad range of reviews rather than focusing on a single extremely negative review, which may be skewed. (In some cases, a review might not even be legitimate, so always weigh each one in relation to other reviews you see.) Also bear in mind that occasionally, personalities simply don't mesh, which we discuss in depth elsewhere in this book, and other things – like weather conditions, permitting delays, and more – may be beyond the control of the professional under consideration. The

WHO SHOULD YOU TRUST?

most critical questions you should consider in a review are those that are not impacted by these things, such as: Did they finish on time, while meeting the agreed upon budget, and with the quality level that the reviewer hoped for? Did they meet the challenges of any unexpected issues that were discovered? Overall, are you satisfied with the end result?

When looking at these reviews, you should check several things. First, make sure they are from projects that are similar is size and scope to yours. After all, there's a huge difference between building a quality deck and constructing a new custom home. You want to be certain that the references you are checking are pertinent to your project so that you are making an apples to apples comparison. Next, make certain they are relatively recent, since much can change over time – from personnel to management. (Bear in mind however that if your general contractor is passionate about your project and expects quality work from his or her tradespeople, a specific trade may change, but the overall quality and passion should remain consistent.)

Show Me the Money!

We saved this one for last, because cost is, unfortunately, where all too many homeowners begin and end their search for a contractor. But price is one of **the last** things you should consider when you are making the decision of who to entrust with your family's dreams and future. Why? Because if a contractor doesn't have the skills, experience, professionalism, integrity and all the other previously mentioned characteristics, what he or she charges won't matter – their lack of the aforementioned traits will end up costing you time, money and aggravation.

All too often, consumers are willing to look at what they believe is the bottom line on a bid and forgive the rest to save a significant amount of money. However, if a company's bid is radically discounted – defined by prices slashed 20 percent or more – than comparable companies, the odds are you'll be getting far more than you bargained for. Radical discounting eventually leads to business suicide for most companies, as they struggle to meet overhead and their financial obligations. "So what?" you may think as a homeowner. "I don't care if company X is around forever – I just want my project done at a great price." Unfortunately, if a company can't pay their own bills, they will cut corners on your project – using substandard materials; cheaper, less experienced tradespeople; and perhaps going out of business before they finish your project. The bottom line is that while it's easy to be emotionally blinded by a good deal, you need to look at exactly what you're getting – and the long-term reliability and stability of the company you're getting it from – for that bargain price.

Now that you know how to find a reliable general contractor or home builder, how do you determine which one is the ideal fit for your family? Read on to find out.

CHAPTER 6

Now, Who Do We *Really* Trust?

Regret #6 Hiring the Wrong Professional

How to weed through your list of qualified professionals to find the one who's right for you.

Do you have a good friend whom you don't see very often, yet every time you get to talk, it's as if you've never been apart? That intangible connection and natural flow of communication between two individuals is key to a long-lasting friendship, but you might not have realized just how important chemistry can be when it comes to selecting a contractor for your remodeling or new custom home construction project. After all, you'll be seeing your contractor on an almost daily basis, and he will be your voice in communicating your vision to all of the individuals who will work on your project. So, ensuring that you and he are able to communicate well and comfortably from your very first meeting is essential. You can't overrate the value of genuinely liking, being able to effectively work with, and respecting the integrity of the person – and the company – to whom you are entrusting your home and dreams.

Yes, selecting a contractor goes far beyond picking someone with a compatible personality. Of course, there are the basics that we covered in the last chapter. Now, we'll assume that you've properly vetted the contractors on your short list and whittled them down to the truly qualified, talented individuals with longstanding diversified experience who are backed by stable companies. So how do you go from the qualified few to the one you choose? What **really** matters?

Over the years, we've found that there are several things our customers *really* want when it comes to selecting a professional remodeling contractor or a new home builder – and some of them might surprise you.

A contractor who listens. There are many qualified professionals out there with strong opinions about how to complete a project. But ultimately, what they want or what's easiest for them shouldn't be the primary objective – what you and your family want and need should be. So, if you have the distinct impression that the contractor you're considering isn't really listening to you, look elsewhere. It is true that since they don't do this everyday, some clients don't have an overall vision for the project but have a few general ideas of what they want. In this case, it's critical to hire a professional GC with good vision for the project, but that vision should be clearly focused on your needs. Once he or she really understands what you are trying to convey, the contractor then must have the ability to clearly articulate your vision to all the various tradespeople, designers and other professionals who will be involved in your project.

A contractor who understands the big picture. An experienced contractor who understands what your family wants will be able to pull from their experience to offer creative solutions to things you might not have even considered. Whether it's moving an appliance to ease kitchen traffic flow, widening doorways to plan for the future, or repositioning windows to allow for better furniture placement, a contractor who understands the entire scope of your project can ensure that its myriad details come together in a cohesive whole.

A contractor with experience. Sure, everyone must get their start somewhere - even great contractors were beginners once – but you don't necessarily want someone learning the right and wrong way to do things on *your* project. There's simply no substitute for having worked in the field for a number of years and having dealt with the challenges that are certain to "pop up." What is most vital is that they have experience in your type of project – whether that's a custom home, kitchen remodel, master suite addition, master bathroom remodel, home addition, renovation or an over-the-garage addition or second-floor addition. Your contractor's experience will allow him to implement creative solutions and will give you a comfort level that he has successfully "been there and done that" in the past.

A contractor who will actually be involved in your project. One of the key questions you should ask when you are interviewing contractors is will the person(s) involved in your initial meetings and planning be working with you throughout the project? This is a great point because some contractors have sales staff handle these initial meetings. Conversely, other companies have an Owner or General Contractor sit in, who is then not involved in the actual day-to-day handling of your project. Obviously, working from Day One with the same person who will actually oversee and coordinate your project (like our clients do when they work with us) reduces the chance for miscommunication. It also eliminates the time-consuming task of staff and clients going back and forth with a go-between.

A contractor who is a skilled manager. Another key question to ask is if the contractor has a strong project management track record. Oftentimes, homeowners are so focused on whether the contractor knows how to build or remodel that they don't think to ask about how he manages the people and processes that are needed to build successfully on either a large or small scale. Managing a good team of handpicked tradespeople, scheduling out who needs to be where when, and planning the smooth progress of each step is crucial to finishing on time and on budget. Let's face it, delays are inevitable on a construction project, generally due to client-initiated project changes, weather, scheduling, and waiting on inspections and/or material availability, but minimizing them and effectively dealing with them can make the difference between finishing on time or not. If a project of this magnitude gets out of control, you as the owner can incur hefty interest charges, possibly lose your rate lock, or potentially pay two mortgages or a mortgage and rent (your existing home or the apartment where you are residing while construction is underway) for longer than you need to.

A contractor who does things right the first time. A contractor who takes the time to understand your needs, conducts thorough planning before the project even starts, and goes the extra mile on the front end will save you incalculable time and money in the long run. Whether it's having the foresight to use durable materials that will minimize long-term maintenance or ensuring that window flashing is installed correctly, it's the details that will make a huge difference in your ultimate satisfaction.

A contractor who communicates. Whether you are living in your home during a home remodeling process or building a new custom home from several states away, keeping the lines of communication open is key to a smooth project. We've successfully worked with several long-distance remodeling and custom home clients and can attest that keeping them in the loop is key to a smooth process. Find a contractor who is committed to communicating both in the manner you prefer – face-to-face, email, texts, phone calls, etc. – and in the frequency your project and peace of mind require, and you'll go a long way toward ensuring a good experience.

NOW, WHO DO WE REALLY TRUST?

A contractor whose judgment you trust. A good dose of common sense is vitally important when it comes to setting priorities. For example, once on a time-critical project, we decided to postpone work for a day because of a predicted torrential downpour. While we could have done interior work that day, we knew that all the tradespeople walking in and out would have created a monumental mess that would have stressed the homeowner and we would have lost even more hours cleaning up. Therefore, a short delay saved time and stress. Because the homeowner trusted our judgment, she didn't agonize over the short delay, and we ultimately finished on time.

A contractor backed by a solid company. First, consider the number of years the company in consideration has been in business. The same logic we mentioned earlier about individual contractors applies to the company. Yes, we do realize that new companies must start somewhere, but seriously consider whether you want your project to be the one that they learn the ropes on.

A contractor involved at every step. The structure we find most effective is having a highly qualified individual involved with a client's project from conception to completion. At Palmer Custom Builders, as a Design-Build Company, the General Contractor is involved from Concept to Completion, along with a Project Coordinator from Construction Start to Completion. Our clients have several key points of contact throughout a project, along with the General Contractor - the Residential Designer, Project Coordinator, Interior Design team and Lead Carpenter. Take the time to ask questions and discover who those points of contact might be, to evaluate how well you can connect with and work with them, and to learn how strongly they share the vision, goals, work ethic and more of the company you are considering. You should also ask the General Contractor and/or Project Coordinator about the skills of their tradespeople - their work ethic and passion for their jobs, and don't be afraid to ask if they would trust them with their own homes.

A contractor who cares. Ultimately, if your builder is passionate about what he does, his love of craftsmanship and detail will translate into your final project and give you much better results.

One final note - never ignore your intuition. If something just doesn't feel right to you – whether it's a contractor who downplays your concerns, ignores your input, talks down to you or anything else – go with your instincts and find someone else. After all, this ultimately is your home and your project; you deserve to work with someone who will care for it – and your family's peace of mind – as much as you do.

CHAPTER 7

Money Matters

Regret #7 Not Getting the Proper Financing in Place or Trading What You Really Want for What You can Afford Right Now

How and when financial considerations should impact your project.

Would you hire a lawyer to defend you in traffic court and not tell him that someone else was driving your car on the day in question? Or would you go to a doctor with a broken arm and not describe your injury, but instead let him run a battery of tests just to discover what was wrong?

As silly as these circumstances sound, all too often homeowners begin a major construction project without divulging critical information to their contractor. Most often, homeowners withhold information unintentionally; they simply forget to mention a previous condition that they believe has been repaired. Why is that information important? Since a contractor can't see through a finished wall, any background a homeowner can provide allows him to make a more informed guess as to what's really going on behind that lovely finish. Knowing that a ceiling once was repaired due to water damage lets him know that he may discover undetected damage when he removes the wall in an adjoining room. This knowledge helps him advise you accordingly, prepares him for what may be ahead, and allows him to build enough time to make a needed correction and work it into the project's timeline.

While such honest mistakes about the history of your home can cause delays, they are nothing compared to the largest "honest" mistake people make with their custom home builder or remodeler: ***Not being upfront about their budget.***

There is a natural reluctance on the part of some homeowners to give a contractor their real "number." That may be because a homeowner genuinely does not know what a new home building or remodeling project will cost, or it might be that they fear an unscrupulous contractor will "find a way" to make their project hit that maximum amount when a smaller amount would suffice. However, that fear is unfounded if you have done your due diligence and selected a reputable, professional contractor.

Just like a doctor or a lawyer, your contractor will work with you to achieve your desired result. Yet just like any other professional, they need critical information going into the project. Consider a kitchen remodel. Your remodeler needs to know if your budget allows for and if you want custom or semi-custom cabinets, which can take 4 weeks or more to arrive. If you want them, your contractor needs to order them early, so they don't cause delays, and you need to budget for custom or semi-custom cabinetry. In a remodel, renovation or new construction project, do you want to include new appliances or work with an existing range or refrigerator that may not have the same counter depth needed for an updated kitchen design? Knowing that on the front end allows for some creative designs and budgeting, while discovering it after a countertop or cabinets are ordered may result in a more costly or unattractive solution and scheduling delays. Understanding what you want and knowing what you can afford will allow your contractor to create a project that fulfills your desires **and** meets your budget. A professional contracting company will carefully guide you through the process of making good design decisions and product selections, while working within a realistic budget with which you both feel comfortable.

But What Happens When You Don't Know What You Can Afford?

The first step in any project is setting a realistic budget. When it comes to new home construction, there are many reliable calculators out there that can tell you how much mortgage a lender **will say** you can afford. Some of the factors they consider are income, debt-to-income ratio, and the size of your down payment. As a rule, lenders say that your monthly housing payment, which they consider to be comprised of principal, interest, taxes and insurance, should be at or less than 28 percent of your income before taxes. Depending on your lender, this may be called the housing ratio or front-end ratio. Then they look at another number that's called the back-end ratio. This number includes all the family's debt commitments – vehicle loans, student loans, and minimum credit card payments – added to the monthly housing payment calculated in the front-end ratio. The rule of thumb is that lenders want to see a back-end ratio of 36 percent or less. However, these numbers are not carved in stone. Federal regulations give legal protection to well-documented mortgages with back-end ratios of as much as 43 percent. Mesh that number with current interest rates and the size of your down payment and you'll see how much lenders **say you can afford** to spend on a new home loan.

For a remodeling project, the process is much the same. We'll get into some general loan parameters later in this chapter, but you'll want to be certain that whether you are refinancing or taking out a line of credit, you can comfortably afford the payments and that they fall within the recommended back-end ratio.

Obviously, there may be a world of difference between what the bank *says* you can afford and what you are comfortable spending on a mortgage or a line of credit. There are a few factors that you'll want to consider whether building new or renovating. The first is that life happens! While you can't plan for the unexpected, you can acknowledge that the unexpected will happen at some point. Whether that's your child getting accepted to that Ivy League school – and the prestigious tuition bill that comes with it – caring for older parents, a job loss, a health scare, or virtually anything else, if you are spending every dime you have on a mortgage, you may be financially vulnerable in the event of an emergency – whether that emergency is positive or negative.

Next – unexpected things happen when you are building or remodeling. Again, these surprises can be good (the countertop material that you really wanted but thought was out of your reach is available and within your budget!) or negative (your contractor encounters unexpected issues when digging a foundation or knocking down a wall in a renovation project). That's why it's essential to build a contingency fund into your project.

In new construction, your contingency fund is typically 5% to 10% of your total project cost. So, for example, if you determine you can comfortably afford to spend $500,000 on a new home, your contingency should be $25,000 to $50,000, which means that you should conservatively be looking at a project cost of around $450,000.

In a remodeling project, most experts recommend a higher contingency – of 5% to 15%, depending on the scope and complexity of your project. How remodeling companies handle contingency funds will vary. For our clients, and with proper planning upfront, contingency funds primarily are needed for the discovery of any "hidden conditions" that could not be addressed in advance because they were unknown, or for homeowner changes or additions to the project. Our homeowners do maintain the freedom to make whatever changes they want during the project, but anything outside of the original construction agreement requires written approval by the homeowner and is captured and paid for by the owner as an Additional Work Authorization. Depending on the nature and cost of the change, payment may be required at the time of Owner's approval of the Additional Work Authorization (which might mean paying for a change out of pocket instead of rolling it into a loan).

It's worth noting that if your contractor or builder is recommending a higher contingency percentage than the standards mentioned above it may indicate that they have done less homework or upfront planning. In remodeling, a higher contingency might be in order if you are dealing with a very complicated, large, older home renovation. In new home construction, it also could be needed in a very large home for which the owners anticipate making some changes along the way or for unexpected building site issues. In the case of a longer planning and construction duration, unexpected world economic factors can come into play, and cause significant pricing fluctuations in building materials. For example, dramatic increases in gas and oil prices or overseas military events can impact the pricing and availability of roofing materials and delivery costs, vinyl siding materials, OSB sheathing and even framing lumber.

How Much Is Too Much?

Now that you have settled on a number that you believe you can comfortably afford. The question becomes: What can I get for what I can afford?

To answer your question reliably, you should begin by working with a qualified professional remodeler or experienced Custom Home Builder. Unlike what you see on reality TV shows (where everything from labor to building supplies to portable restrooms may be donated or deeply discounted) there are many factors that go into determining how much home you can expect to get for your budget that go far beyond basic cost per square foot calculators. A professional can help you take a realistic look at your lot, your plans, or your existing home and tell you what you can get for your budget. What's more, they may refer you to a Real Estate Professional for guidance on what you *should* spend on a home in the location you're looking at to keep in line with surrounding homes. (The old real estate adage still applies that you don't want to have the most expensive home in the neighborhood.)

What Kind of Loan Should I Get?

Once you know roughly how much you can afford and what you can get for it, the question then becomes how you finance it. While you'll want to talk with a qualified lender to learn which loan is best for you and your individual financial circumstances (at last count, there were more than 200 types of loans out there!), here are some generalities:

New Construction Loans

Construction-to-permanent loans are the most popular ways to finance new home construction. These loans work when your lender advances funds to your builder to pay for construction. Once the home is completed, your lender rolls the balance of the loan into a standard mortgage. With construction-to-permanent loans, there is only one closing, which saves you money, and you generally have the option to lock in interest rates early in the process. (Which can save you money in the long run if you think interest rates will increase before your home is complete.) On the downside, because there is not a constructed home (to use as collateral) down payment requirements tend to be higher, with most lenders requiring 20%, although some may accept a 10% down payment in certain circumstances.

Stand-alone construction loans are the other alterative. In these loans, the lender fronts your builder the money to pay for the construction of your home. Once the home is built, you secure a mortgage to pay the loan balance. These loans require less of a down payment, which might make them more attractive on the front end, but there are two closings – one on the construction loan, and one on the final mortgage (and thus, double closing costs). What's more, since you are not locking in your rate on the front end, you run the danger of seeing it increase (if you are building in a time when rates are fluid).

Regardless of which type of loan you choose, one mistake some people make is finding the perfect lot and grabbing it before they are financially ready to build or have made a final decision on the type of home to build. The home plan they ultimately decide upon might not be right for the land/lot they've already purchased. In some cases, getting a lot loan may damage your financial ability to build the home of your dreams. That's because lot loans typically require a high down payment (around 20% but they can go as high as 50%), which eats away at your savings, and higher interest rates, since you are financing unimproved property that lenders feel you may have an incentive to walk away from if you are faced with financial difficulties. If your ability to afford a new custom home is borderline, having that much cash tied up in a lot loan can damage it. With that being said, there are some lenders that offer short-term lot loans of a few years (instead of 5, 10 or 20 year) that might work well to roll into a construction loan.

Remodeling Loans

When it comes to remodeling, there are multiple finance options, including financing it out of pocket (which might be an option for a small renovation project), mortgage refinancing, home equity loans, cash out refinancing, or a home equity line of credit.

There are even a few federal government options for new homebuyers who go into a home requiring a remodeling project. (Of course, talk with your lender to see if your home qualifies for these or other renovation loan programs.) The Federal Housing Administration's

Streamlined 203(k) is one of the more popular renovation loan programs. It permits homebuyers to finance as much as an additional $35,000 into their mortgage to improve or upgrade a home before they move in. Renovation loans are generally used to update or improve a house or condominium needing essential repairs, such as new wiring or plumbing, weatherization, lead-based paint stabilization or abatement, roof replacement, kitchen and bath renovation or space reconfiguring, or interior upfits.

Other renovation programs like the Fannie Mae HomeStyle® Renovation Mortgage offer higher loan limits for more extensive projects. The HomeStyle Renovation Mortgage allows borrowers to finance improvements of up to 50% of the as-completed value of the home with a first mortgage, while offering lower rates than second mortgages, home equity lines, or credit card debt. Another plus is that this loan allows homeowners to finance "luxury" items, such as swimming pools, major additions, sunrooms and outdoor living spaces.

For existing homes, mortgage refinancing and cash out refinancing are popular options. These allow you to use the equity you have built up in your home and spend it on a remodeling project. While you do have to pay closing costs, you might be able to save in the long run if the new interest rate is lower than your original rate.

Home equity lines of credit are appealing options for remodeling projects because interest rates tend to be lower (since the line of credit is secured by the equity in your home) and homeowners can deduct the interest on their taxes. Plus, you can generally pay these off on your own timetable (if you meet monthly minimum payments), allowing you to pay off debt more quickly.

One key consideration with any of these programs is that you don't want to be paying for a remodeling project longer than you'll be enjoying its benefits. For example, if a new refrigerator typically lasts for

10 years, you don't want to end up financing it for 20 years.

There are other methods out there, but they tend to be more complex and may end up costing you more in the long run (borrowing on credit cards, taking a loan from your 401K, Reverse Mortgages, etc.) Remember, obtaining the proper loan for your financial situation can save you on interest rates, get a lower down payment, and ultimately get you in the house you want.

When Is the Time Right?

Despite the many financial options out there, you and your family must carefully consider what you want and what you can realistically afford. You may find yourself in a situation that you simply want more from a new home, remodeling, renovation or addition project than you can afford at the time, and that's when waiting – although difficult – is well worth it to get what you ultimately want. Although a professional remodeler can help you phase in your project over time, bear in mind that by doing so, you will pay more in the long run. That's true simply because tradespeople will have to come to your site not just once, but twice, material prices and interest rates may increase over time, you may have to temporarily complete something that you'll later have to demolish or alter in the next phase, etc. Oftentimes waiting for what you really want is better than settling for cutting corners on an investment in your family's future.

CHAPTER 8

Listen Up!

Regret #8 Not Listening to the Professional You Hired

*How to work with the professionals you hire
to get to where you need to be.*

You've done your due diligence, hired the right contractor and established a realistic budget. Now, all that's left is to sit back, relax and watch as your project is completed before your eyes – right? If only it were that simple! The fact of the matter is that one of the most critical aspects of any project – whether it's a small remodel, a major renovation or a brand-new custom home – is you and how you work with the professional you've hired.

Consider some homeowners we know who had always envisioned exactly how their kitchen remodeling project would look. They had pictured the configuration of the appliances, the layout of the kitchen island, the fixtures, the hardware, all down to the most minute detail. They then brought in numerous contractors and asked them to quote the exact configuration they required. What they didn't do is ask those professionals for their design recommendations. When we were approached about the project, we offered some suggestions – based

LISTEN UP!

on our experience – for how the kitchen could be better designed to make the most effective use of the available space. If the client had steadfastly pursued their initial plans – or went with a contractor who quoted their project "as is" – they eventually would have been very disappointed, because that design would not have maximized their investment or the room's functionality.

As these clients and many others discover, listening to the experienced professionals you hire makes all the difference in your results. Drawing upon his experience of what has worked in the field and in real family homes during previous projects, a professional can offer suggestions or alterations that have a tremendous impact. Instead of just building "to plan," a design/build firm is going to ensure that the plan will work on all levels – structural, aesthetic, functional and budgetary. They'll suggest changes like making certain that windows are symmetrically placed to improve a traditional home's façade or relocating a fireplace to open up a room addition, improve a view, or make sure the TV placement flows with the seating area.

Being open to these suggestions, however, is key to a successful project. Ultimately, that choice is up to you as a customer and the homeowner. But what exactly makes one a good listener? Should you as a customer blindly acquiesce to every suggestion your contractor makes? Here are some tips we have learned over the years from realistic customers that might help you better relate to and understand the professionals you hire.

It goes without saying that before you take someone's advice, you must respect them and their expertise. If you have gone through the proper process to vet and then select a qualified professional contractor, you should honor that professional's ability, experience and time just as you expect your contractor to respect your time and business. This mutual respect and trust are the foundation for a strong working relationship that can steer you through the good times and ease the inevitable bumps inherent in a long construction process.

As we discussed in the last chapter, being upfront and honest about your project's scope and budget with your contractor on the front end will save you money, time and heartache. Now that your contractor understands your budget, be certain to listen to them as they make suggestions with that budget in mind. A professional contractor understands that several factors and material selections can dramatically impact a project's cost, and they will work with you to meet your desired budget, if it is realistic. Does that mean that you must sacrifice that quartz countertop you just fell in love with because your contractor says the cost is too high? Not necessarily – if you are willing to sacrifice in other areas. That's where honesty, openness and listening come in. If he knows those must-have items that you *really* want – as opposed to what you would just like to have if it happens to be possible – your contractor may be able to offer alternatives that would reduce costs in other areas to make up for the overage in the one that really matters to you. However, if you just ignore your contractor's professional budgetary cautions on selection after selection, you can quickly place yourself in a deep financial bind.

That holds true not just with the cost of options, but with the time it may take to acquire those options as well. Remember that in addition to what you see being accomplished on the jobsite, there is lots of hands-on activity occurring behind the scenes; materials are being selected and ordered, follow through and follow-up contact with vendors and product deliveries are being coordinated, and timelines with tradesmen are being planned and scheduled. If you suddenly decide you must have a product that takes three times as long a lead time to acquire, your project may be delayed. No one expects a homeowner to be a construction expert; it's the responsibility of your contractor to establish a clear understanding of your project's procedures, phases and timetable and to explain how your selections will impact that timeline. (We at Palmer Custom Builders®, for example, provide clients with a detailed Remodeling and New Construction Guide when appropriate for their project). Yet realistic customers strive to grasp what is important and be aware of what needs to happen when, and to understand the impact that decisions they make – or decisions they delay – will have on the process. In fact, realistic customers almost universally can be decisive once presented with the facts. When it comes to selecting materials or making a critical decision, the homeowner's ability to make timely, informed decisions will keep a project on track.

Together with that honesty goes open-mindedness and flexibility. Being open to learning about new ideas, whether it's a new product or a new way of looking at things, is essential. A remodeling or new construction project is a complicated, technical undertaking involving many details and phases both on the jobsite and behind the scenes. The one constant in these projects is **change.** Some phases will progress faster than planned while unforeseen issues inevitably will appear during a project. Common causes of delays, like weather, material backorders, and scheduling necessary building inspections, can be nerve-wracking for homeowners and contractors. However, if you keep your mind on the ultimate goal and realize that some time shift is normal, you won't get bogged down in minutia and lose sight of the big picture. Listening as your contractor explains the reasons behind movement in the schedule is key to preserving a good working relationship.

It goes without saying that a willingness to listen does not mean blindly following. A willingness on the part of the homeowner to ask questions is vital. If you don't understand something, you should never be afraid to ask questions until you have clarity. A true professional should never have an issue with explaining the reason for something. Keeping concerns to yourself only hinders communication and can build resentment.

The ultimate payoff of listening to the professionals you hire is having a great experience. You'll feel good about the project; it will become exciting and fun instead of stressful; and everyone involved will be proud of and happy about the job - which means your results will be spectacular!

CHAPTER 9

The Devil Really Is in the Details

Regret #9 Rushing Through Without Proper Planning

Step back, take a deep breath, and dive into the details on the front end.

You have your contractor; you have your financing; you have your plans; and you are more than ready to get going on this remodeling, renovation, addition, custom home or home improvement project you've been dreaming about for so long. But before the first nail is hammered or the first cubic yard of concrete is poured, you should take a step back to look at the overall picture of your project and to make certain that all the details make sense for your family.

Why? Because it's much easier, less expensive and *possible* to make adjustments before you begin construction. Take the case of one homeowner we know who had constructed a beautiful outdoor living area. The stone fireplace was meticulously and expertly crafted, the seating area was generously sized and well planned. In fact, almost every aspect of their space was perfect. Except for the glaring electrical outlet built into the front of their stone fireplace that stuck out like a sore thumb. With just a little forethought, these homeowners easily could have moved the outlet to a less visible yet still functional location. Redoing this small but glaring detail after the fact would have been incredibly expensive and time consuming, as it would have required undoing and redoing stonework as well as moving electrical lines that at that point were buried under pavers and stone. Taking the time – and giving your contactor the necessary time – to step back and review your near-final plans with a fresh set of eyes may help eliminate potential pitfalls like the one these homeowners experienced.

But how can you avoid every pitfall? The truth is, you can't foresee every possible issue that might crop up, but dealing with a qualified professional contractor reduces your chances of making the same mistakes others have made. An experienced contractor has seen things in the field – and made those last-minute changes as needed – so they have a wealth of experience from which to draw.

Your contractor also has experience with what former clients wish they had done. Often as people live in their homes, they inevitably realize what they should have done or what they would have done differently if they had the opportunity. In the hopes of preventing some future angst, we've compiled a list of some tension points that homeowners frequently mention to us when they are looking to build a new custom home, remodel, add to, or renovate their existing homes. These are great things to consider now if you are planning a remodeling project or new custom-built home of your own. After all, it's been said that learning from experience is intelligence, but learning from the experience of others is wisdom.

Kitchens That Are Cooking

The best advice we have ever heard when designing a kitchen is simply to plan for the way you *really* cook. That may mean splurging a bit for upgrades on the appliances that you'll *actually* use or stealing square footage from an adjoining room to secure the space you need – particularly if there are multiple cooks or young chefs in training in

THE DEVIL REALLY IS IN THE DETAILS

your home. That could also mean designing a simple but functional kitchen if you prefer to eat out. The main key here is to make your kitchen work for you, and not allow current design trends, the idealized dreams of a celebrity chef, or the go-to sketches of a kitchen designer to circumvent your actual needs.

If you are planning to include an island in your kitchen, make it function for you. The addition of a sink – or even a secondary sink – transforms this area into a real workhorse. Add a drawer microwave and/or dishwasher to ease traffic flow around the perimeter counters. In existing homes, we're frequently tearing out multilevel island surfaces and replacing them with single-level countertops. This provides an efficient work surface for cooking or homework, and more room for comfortable seating and entertaining, which in turn visually opens up the space.

When it comes to materials, think about the long haul and how they will endure. Believe it or not, those seemingly indestructible stainless steel sinks do get scratches and dings. The thicker the sink (they typically range from 18 gauge to 23 gauge), the less likely it is to be damaged. A small difference in quality (about a $250 upgrade) will make a huge difference in durability and sound elimination. The same thinking applies to sinks made from composite materials or porcelain – invest in quality.

Think carefully about every appliance choice - even the seemingly minor ones. A stronger and quieter garbage disposal, for example, speeds kitchen cleanup and reduces noise issues when family living areas are open to the kitchen. (No one wants to hear the disposal while they are trying to watch a game!)

If you're remodeling or renovating, switch out a dated double oven to a newer model (or add one in the first place) to provide needed flexibility. Since many older double ovens were too tiny to accommodate large cookie sheets, an upgrade gives you the oven space you need when entertaining while saving your back on a daily basis. While we're on the subject, switching out an existing electric range for a new gas model isn't as costly as many people assume, and it can make a huge difference to the cook in the family.

Oftentimes when renovating a kitchen, homeowners will replace their refrigerator even if the existing one is still functioning to improve its appearance, features and efficiency. If that is your plan, consider running a new electric line out to the garage and install the old refrigerator there. This secondary fridge provides room for beverages and bulky, seasonal or entertaining items for which you never seem to have enough refrigerator space inside.

Resist trends unless it's very important to you – particularly with things that are built in and costly, such as countertops and appliances. Here's a great case in point. Pot fillers – faucets that extend out over a cook top, ostensibly to fill large pasta pots. These features are still quite trendy and appear in many magazines, but they might not be practical for everyone. (Because you incur the cost of running an extra water line and a costly pot filler faucet for a feature you might not use frequently.) So while these trends are important to some homeowners, factor in the cost and make sure it's something you actually want instead of something you just feel you should have because it's the latest trend.

Another huge pressure point is kitchen cabinets and drawers. Make certain that there are enough and that they are spacious enough to accommodate all your dishes, utensils and favorite pots and pans, such as oversized cookie sheets, pressure cookers or slow cookers, casserole dishes, and more. If you have a beloved collection, you might want to consider displaying it prominently behind glass doors or on open shelving, but beware of using too much glass or open shelving if the inside of your cabinets tends toward the messy or mismatched. These showcase cabinets or open shelves are wonderful focal points in kitchens with tall ceilings – where you can place treasures that are beautiful and rarely used up high and out of harm's way. Also, plan for key cabinet accessories on the front end, such as Lazy Susan's in corners, large deep roll out drawers, pull out shelves, and hidden compartments for garbage and recycling containers and storage solutions for smart technology.

Remember that counter space is also critical. Realistically think about how many appliances you'll be keeping in plain view and where they will be placed. If you use your toaster every morning or your blender every afternoon, plan for it to have a permanent place to call its own. Make certain that there's enough clearance under wall cabinets and any shelves to accommodate the proper usage of your favorite coffee pot, mixer or sandwich maker.

Make certain there are plentiful electrical outlets and that they are strategically placed where you will need them. Continuous plug mold is a strip of electrical outlets, spaced out every 12 inches, that's tucked underneath the edge of upper cabinets. This puts a concealed electrical connection everywhere you really need and eliminates the need for unsightly outlets in your beautiful new kitchen backsplash.

Finally, think carefully about task and ambient light and add under-cabinet LED task lighting in critical areas.

Bathrooms as Sanctuaries

Likewise, when it comes to this private sanctuary, plan for the way **you** want to use your master bathroom. Separate vanities are a must if two people are sharing the space. Many homeowners will bow to tradition and invest in a costly and elaborate garden tub, only to realize they never use it. Likewise, some homeowners went with the steam shower trend that was popular a few years ago without fully grasping their maintenance issues. In these homes, we're often taking out the tub and/or an old tiled steam shower and replacing them with a spacious walk-in shower complete with niches, built in shelves, benches and multiple shower heads - fixed and handheld.

Speaking of niches, there should be at least one extra-large niche, or two large niches, built into every shower so that bathers have a place for necessities. Niches can be installed in locations to keep products out of sight lines and eliminate the need for shower caddies. Self-draining corner shelves are a great option, too.

All too often, contractors may replace the showerhead without raising it when they are remodeling, renovating or building a new bathroom. Since they may be removing the tile, drywall, etc. anyway, raising plumbing lines by a few inches is a very minimal expense. The difference in how the shower feels – particularly for tall people who previously have had to bend down to wash their hair – is amazing!

Showers themselves have a lot of issues if you stick with tradition and don't think outside the box. Tiling all the way to the ceiling in a shower is more hygienic (ever looked at the gunk that accumulates on top of that top row of tile?), eases cleaning, visually enlarges the space, and makes it feel more finished.

Likewise, don't settle for builder basics when it comes to toilets. The new higher commodes are 18" – the same height as a dining room chair. This 2" lift (standard height is 16") makes all the difference for a person of average height, for older people who may have difficulty bending, and for those of any age who just need a little extra assistance.

Don't forget to plan for the future. You might not want to install grab bars in the shower or by the commode if you don't need them yet, but if you plan on making this your forever home, you can have your contractor build the necessary bracing into the walls to make adding safety features a snap when the time does come. Likewise, plan an

THE DEVIL REALLY IS IN THE DETAILS

easy-access shower, wide doorways and a graciously sized space to accommodate any medical equipment that you or a loved one might need at some point down the road.

Finally, don't neglect lighting and ventilation. Whether you are building new or remodeling, choose lighting options that are bright enough to avoid late night collisions with walls or trips over slippers but not wake your loved ones as they sleep or blind you with glare. Make certain that there's enough light placed at the right location to apply makeup or to shave comfortably. While you are replacing lighting in a renovation or remodeling project, take a look at your bath fan. More efficient and quieter bathroom exhaust fans are a needed upgrade in most older homes.

Everything Else

Make certain that every room in your home is functional and the spaces flow well. Separate family rooms, living rooms and dining rooms might look nice on a plan, but many people are doing away with compartmentalized spaces and adding larger multipurpose rooms. However, if you have loud teenagers – or a spouse who likes to cheer on their favorite team – you may want to consider one area that can be closed off. Again, the key is to determine your needs first.

Small spaces tend to create some of the largest problems. Planning for properly sized and functional mudrooms, drop zones, laundry rooms and pantries makes a huge difference in how you use your home – and how often you must nag kids and spouses about putting things away. If you are renovating, replace outdated wire pantry shelves – the kind that break under the weight of canned goods or that items fall through. Solid shelving designed to accommodate the types of items you store (dedicated space for tall items, etc.) will allow you to clearly see and easily access what you have on hand.

In most areas of the country, if you can budget 20-30% more than the cost of a screened porch, opt for a sunroom instead of a screened porch, you'll be much happier long-term. Even in southern states where the climate is warm enough to get a lot of use out of a screened porch, you still can't use it year round. A little heat in the winter and AC in the summer make a huge difference in comfort. Another consideration: Spring and fall pollen means that you'll be cleaning up often, and those who suffer from allergies might not be able to use the space during these peak pollen times.

No matter which room you are considering, choose timeless classics. Natural materials like granite, marble, slate and man-made quartz, as well as neutral carpet palettes that can be updated with simple splashes of color, will always outlast the trend of the moment. Think about the beautiful spaces of homes that have endured and then ask yourself if you really think you'll still want to live with that orange laundry room floor or blue washer and dryer in five years.

In the end, carefully considering every detail of your renovation, remodel, addition or new custom home project and how it will both stand the test of time and serve your family over the long run will help you avoid mistakes.

CHAPTER 10

Are You Going Through a Phase?

Regret #10 Not Properly Planning How to Phase in Your Project

What to consider when you can't do everything all at once.

If you look at our culture today, it seems we Americans have an almost innate tendency to want it all – and to want it **now**. We desire fast luxury cars that get great gas mileage. We expect our children to excel academically while simultaneously covering their bedroom walls with sports medals. We crave foods that taste great while being healthy. So why would we expect anything different when it comes to our home remodeling, home renovation, addition or new home construction projects?

The truth is, there are some very good reasons to phase in a project over time. By far, the number one reason most people do so is budgetary. Homeowners often will seek to phase in an extensive project rather than stretching their family finances beyond the point where they are comfortable. This makes perfect sense because in theory, instead of cutting corners and sacrificing the aspects of your project that you really want, you can have it all – if you have the patience to wait for it.

For example, your ultimate dream might be remodeling an outdated kitchen to create a gourmet's dream and opening up the space to a gracious outdoor living area that includes a sunroom, expanded deck and a pool. But you might not have the financial resources to complete everything at once. At that point, you'd be weighing decisions like downsizing your dreams for the kitchen and opting for lower quality cabinets, appliances and surface materials, scrapping the pool altogether, or sacrificing the sunroom. If you're simply willing to delay gratification for some time, you might be able to have it all. (It goes without saying that you'll want to discuss your personal situation with a trusted banker or other financial advisor before you make any final decisions on financing a project. Some decisions you make on financing might impact your ability to secure another loan down the road, so consult with them first and be honest and open about your future plans.)

Other reasons for phasing in a project may be purely personal. You might have growing children you anticipate moving out or aging parents you anticipate moving in. You may be planning for your own retirement or a new addition to your family. You might be planning to work from home in the future. In these cases, you might be thinking of a transitional project – completing only what needs to be done now and then waiting to see how your life changes will dictate the next steps. Your reasons also could be seasonal, such as wanting to complete a kitchen remodel before the holidays so you can host family and friends but not wanting the adjoining family and living rooms that you'd eventually like to open up to be in disarray while you are entertaining.

Regardless of the reasons for phasing in a project, making certain that you proceed in a logical order is key to your success and future happiness.

First, as always, you want to make certain that you are working with a qualified, professional contractor who has completed projects like yours in the past. Thoroughly discuss this with your contractor and remember in custom building no two projects are alike, but there are a lot of commonalities. The skillset and knowledge required to phase in a project properly goes above and beyond the norm. Their approach must be forward thinking enough to understand what needs to happen at some indeterminate time in the future, and they must determine how to best accommodate your current plans and those future needs.

Next, you must be open and honest about all your plans. Tell your contractor exactly what you are hoping to achieve in the future and when you realistically hope to achieve it. This allows your contractor to keep the big picture in mind no matter which phase they are currently working on.

Then, be willing to listen to their advice. Once you tell the contractor what you hope to create and the resources you have to spend right now, they may surprise you – in either a good or a bad way. For example, you might have decided that you want to put in your outdoor living area right away and hold off on the pool. Your contractor may take a realistic look at your backyard and explain that the heavy equipment needed to install your pool would irreparably damage the landscaping and living area you hoped to build first. In that case, you might have to go back to the drawing board to create a plan that makes sense.

On the flip side, they may tell you that it would be more cost-effective to do something now instead of later. For example, you may have wanted to install new flooring in a new breakfast room but planned to hold off on refinishing the floors in the adjoining family room. While you have the flooring people on site, it might cost less and be far less chaotic to have that entire piece of the project completed at once. A contractor who is entrusted with the complete scope of your project can draw from their experience to make practical recommendations like these.

They also will understand the complexities that need to happen behind the scenes. They will know which electrical and plumbing lines need to be run now so that they can easily be pulled or tapped into later. They will grasp whether it makes sense to provide for gas line connectivity to a future outdoor kitchen while they are running lines for a current kitchen remodel. They can advise you on how to select landscaping that won't be destroyed by future construction and have a handle on what items you can live with being in a "partially finished" state depending on the timing of your next phase of construction.

Your contractor should also be able to help you understand the costs of phasing your project in over time. In many cases, it may cost more to spread things out, which makes sense if you consider the economies of scale that come from a larger project. For example, if you have to have drywall crews come out once for the kitchen in Phase 1, then again to redo a recently opened family room wall in Phase 2, you'll probably end up paying a little more than if you did it all at once, since they will have to come to your site, unload and reload materials, set up, etc. twice instead of once. The same applies for all the other trades who will be enlisted in the completion of your project. Oftentimes, the needed flexibility of doing things over time makes up for these additional costs, but you should understand and weigh the costs carefully to ensure that phasing in a project is a wise choice for you.

Finally, listen to your contractor and any other professionals you work with when it comes to making selections for phased in projects. If you want the continuity that comes from the same materials, you'll want to stick with tried and true colors, materials and resources. For example, if you want the same style of faucet that you are installing in your kitchen island this year to grace your outdoor bar two years down the road, you'll want to select a model that is not likely to be discontinued or purchase two now to avoid the issue entirely. The same logic applies for everything from decking and siding materials to countertop and flooring.

It goes without saying that things will change over time – particularly if you are phasing in your project over several years. Instead of being locked into your original ideas, be open to changes. Many folks for example, may have envisioned phasing in a dedicated media room over their garage when those spaces were all the rage a few years back. Today, advances in technology have all but made those theatre rooms with bulky projectors and wall screens obsolete. They are now using those spaces for guest suites, areas for visiting children or aging parents, home offices, hobby rooms or more. Be open to changes in technology, building materials, and even outdoor living trends that ultimately can make your project better than you initially envisioned.

It also goes without saying, but we'll mention it here anyway, that the best-case scenario involves using the same contractor throughout all the phases of your project. Why? Because they will know your project from the inside out, knowing exactly where all your home's skeletons are buried – and by that we mean everything from where utility lines were connected to what's inside your walls, any issues or obstacles they faced in the initial round of construction, and intangibles such as how best to communicate with you and your family's unique taste, needs, and requirements.

Even if you do plan on using the same contractor throughout the project, have them document everything that they did in the initial and subsequent phases of work – just in case. Particularly if your project is being stretched out over several years, there is always the possibility that Building Codes will change, personnel may leave, procedures may evolve, or the company you initially hired may no longer be in business. One way we at Palmer Custom Builders® handle this is by creating a digital photo file of the construction process of every project we complete – not just for phased in projects where it is essential. This digital reference is a wonderful tool for us and tradesmen to use as we are going through the construction process, because it allows everyone involved to see exactly what has been done in prior steps.

In the end, proper planning and documentation can bring every phase of your project together into a beautiful and cohesive whole.

CHAPTER **11**

Are We There Yet?

Regret #11 My Choices Delayed My Project

How to keep your project running on time and on budget.

Let's face it: We all make poor choices at some point in our lives. Maybe it was that outfit or hairstyle that you should have left back in the 80s. Perhaps it was that questionable dating choice that you are still regretting. The place where you don't want to make poor decisions is on your home remodeling, renovation or new construction project, because unlike a bad haircut, you'll have to live with the consequences of your construction decisions for years – or even decades – to come.

Unfortunately, that realization can have a chilling effect on some homeowners, who then become hesitant to make decisions. Which is a shame. Because ultimately, the speed and efficiency with which you as a homeowner make decisions is one of the few aspects of your project over which you have complete and total control. Think about it. You can't control the monsoon rains that delay digging footers or how quickly your local building inspector manages to work your home in during a critical phase. You can't control how efficiently your general contractor schedules his or her subs. (Although if you've done your due diligence on the front end, you've selected a GC who has enough experience and a good enough relationship with the trades involved in your project to speed this process along.)

In fact, the list of things that are beyond your influence is enough to give a migraine to a control freak. But if you have selected a professional, experienced General Contractor, you shouldn't worry about them. That's his or her job – and they've done it hundreds of times before.

What you should focus on is your role in the process – which is making critical decisions about the shape, scope and style of your project. The best way to accomplish that is to take the time to sit down with your contractor on the front end and really listen as he or she explains the process and the timeline.

After all, no one expects a homeowner to be a construction expert; it's the responsibility of your contractor to establish a clear understanding of your project's procedures, phases and timetable. (We at Palmer Custom Builders®, for example, spend time with every client at the beginning of the project getting everyone on the same page. When it's appropriate for the type of project, we also provide clients with a detailed, written Remodeling and New Construction Guide.)

Scope and timelines should be firmly established in these initial meetings. Why? Because once demolition and/or construction begins, changing things becomes time consuming and costly. For example, if you originally decided that you were perfectly fine with a wall separating your kitchen from your family room, your contractor made plans to build that wall per specifications. You might walk into your new kitchen as it's under construction and realize that it feels too closed in, and thus, you want that wall removed. This seemingly small change can have major implications. If it's a load-bearing wall, your contractor may have to go back to the drawing board and consult with a structural engineer to re-engineer your plans for removing a wall. It might require reinforcing other walls and beams or changing the bracing and joists on the floor above, which might require tearing into an already completed second floor. Adding support piers in your crawl space or under a concrete slab may even be needed. They may have to reroute any utility and HVAC lines that were planned to be in that wall. Cabinets may need to be reconfigured to give you ample space – and possibly re-ordered, which can cause extensive delays. That throws tradesmen and inspection schedules into turmoil as they must be pushed back and then rescheduled. All this from a seemingly "minor" homeowner change to the scope of a project.

Now, we're not saying that you shouldn't make any changes. There are times when scope changes are essential – particularly in a remodeling or renovation project. Your contractor may discover an unexpected utility line in the walls, extensive wood rot or structural damage, or any of myriad other issues that should be addressed for your family's safety and peace of mind. If you've selected a qualified professional contractor, they will take much of this burden from you by thoroughly examining all the options *before* they start to finalize the project's scope. The beauty of working with a professional is that they have the experience to see the full potential of your project and its likely pitfalls and explain them to you on the front end.

There are also times when changes are essential for your family's happiness. If you realize when you see your new kitchen beginning to take shape that it is in fact too congested with a wall, making the scope change to open up the space during the initial construction project will most likely prevent an expensive remodeling project in the all-too-near future. But you should be aware of the extra cost in both time and money that your decision to make the change will incur and not be upset with your contractor because of the results. Oftentimes, families will decide that their ultimate happiness outweighs the short-term discomfort of a longer and/or more costly project.

On a seemingly more minor scale are the countless decisions you'll need to make about everything from fixtures to flooring to paint colors. Some of these choices will undoubtedly be easy, since you've probably spent a great deal of time envisioning exactly how you want your project to look. Not to worry though ... professional contractors will have design pros available to assist you through every step of the way, whether you need a little or a lot of assistance in making these important decisions. However, some of these choices will inevitably be tougher to make. It's these decisions we'd like you to focus on right now.

Let's imagine that you went to the stone warehouse to select the material for your kitchen countertops. While you're there, you see a much more exotic and unique (read expensive) natural material that you fall in love with. You desperately want to change your plans and specify this material instead, but it costs about 33% more than what you originally budgeted.

When faced with a difficult decision like this, we strongly encourage you to consult with your contactor. Here's why: A Professional Contractor understands that several factors and material selections can dramatically impact a project's cost and will work with you to meet your desired budget and timeline, if it is realistic. Your contractor can investigate the details of your new countertop material and give you a realistic picture of how selecting it will impact your budget and your project timeline. It may be that your contractor can advise you on simple ways to make up the cost overage in other areas, such as selecting less expensive plumbing fixtures or a lower cost flooring alternative. He or she may discover that the material you want is readily available and won't impact your timeline – or he may discover that since it's an exotic material, turnaround times may be double or triple the norm, which would alter your schedule dramatically. (Remember that in addition to what you see being accomplished on the jobsite, there is lots of hands-on activity occurring behind the scenes; materials are being selected and ordered, follow through and follow-up contact with vendors and product deliveries are being coordinated, and timelines with tradesmen are being planned and scheduled.)

Remember that your contractor has your best interests at heart. He or she wants you to be happy with your project, both for their own personal satisfaction with a job well done and because happy customers ultimately lead to referrals. They want to work with you. If you open up to them and discuss the difficult choices, you'll be able to get through them more quickly, efficiently and with all the necessary information you need to make a wise decision.

CHAPTER **12**

Expect the Unexpected

Regret #12 Not Planning for the Unexpected

How to deal with the contingencies that will show up in your project.

There's an old saying that goes, "If you want to make God laugh, tell Him your plans." Perhaps nowhere does this humorous adage hold truer then when it comes to new construction or remodeling projects.

That's because, as the other saying goes, "Stuff Happens!" That's not to say that it's bad stuff. Some wonderful unexpected things often pop up during the course of a home remodeling, addition, renovation or custom home project. Yet no matter whether the inevitable surprises are good or bad, they require the proper frame of mind and the financial reserves to maximize their value and minimize their impact. Here are a few of the unexpected surprises that may occur in your project – and how to deal with them.

Attitude Is Everything

As we talked about in earlier chapters, the two most important things that impact your project are your attitude and the contractor you select to handle your project. Let's talk about you first.

EXPECT THE UNEXPECTED

Construction is exciting! Whether you are building your dream home from scratch or turning the house you live in today into a home that will fulfill all your family's needs tomorrow, this is truly an exciting time filled with tremendous possibilities. While it might be normal to be a little apprehensive about a project of this magnitude, your excitement should far outweigh your stress. Excited and happy homeowners are much better able to handle whatever challenges construction throws at them, because they can take things in stride. If you are not excited about your project and its possibilities, that's a huge warning sign that something is not right – whether it's financing, plans, timing, contractor, or something else.

Also, as we talked about earlier, a good professional relationship with your contractor based on mutual respect is essential. Think about it: If challenges arise, you want to be certain that the person you are asking to handle them is someone whose opinion you value and whose expertise you trust. If you view your contractor as "just a hired hand," instead of a competent professional, you've either hired the wrong contractor or have the wrong attitude going into a project. In either case, you could find yourself facing huge difficulties if or when unforeseen events arise. Think of your contractor as a professional in the same way you think of your lawyer or your doctor. You may not have an intimate understanding of the law or medicine, but you trust that these professionals do. Certainly, you may take a proactive approach to your health and legal situation – whether that entails proofing legal documents or checking the side effects and drug interaction precautions on prescription medicines – but you still have a level of trust in the opinions of these professionals. That same type of professional courtesy should be extended to your contractor when they inform you that the railing that you fell in love with has to be altered to meet current building code or that the counter surface material you desire won't hold up under daily use. Just like the other professionals in your life, your contractor can help you work through the diagnosis to find a cure – if you work with them to do so.

Finances Are Everything Else!

Okay, money isn't the actual heart of your project, but it does flow through your project's veins. That's why having sound financing that has a solid built-in contingency fund is essential to your project's success.

In Chapter 7, we talked in detail about how much of a contingency fund you should have. To recap, in new construction, it's typically 5% to 10% of your total project cost. In a remodeling project, most experts recommend a higher contingency – of 5% to 15%, depending on the scope and complexity of your project. This contingency fund is a cushion that can help your project survive a financial hit – whether the reason for the unexpected blow is positive or negative.

What are some of the things that you'd need to dive into your contingency funds for? Unexpected soil issues when you are digging footings and foundations in a new construction or remodeling project are a major and frequent reason for having to use contingency fund dollars. In remodeling, unexpected issues behind the walls are a large reason for using contingency funds. (Just think of those home shows you see on TV, where water leaking through a faulty upstairs window frame runs down the interior of a first-floor wall and rots it out, without the homeowners realizing that the damage has occurred.) While some of these issues may be covered under your contract, others such as "Hidden Conditions" (issues "hidden" behind the walls, the roof or the ceiling in a remodeling project or beneath the soil in a new construction project) will not be, so it's always best to plan for the worst - especially in older homes or where potential past substandard work may have been performed.

Yet the main reason that contingency funds are tapped into is for owner-initiated changes to the scope of your project. Here are a few examples of how that can happen. Say you are building your new custom home and planned for an open grilling and entertaining deck to save on costs.

As you walk the property during construction, you notice that the deck gets full afternoon sun, which would make it nearly unbearable in the summer months. Construction is the time to change that. Your contractor should be able to offer options for covering the space, ranging from extending the roof to adding awnings or even a pergola. Building a covering and supports is much more cost-effective during construction than after, since you won't have to demolish something that is already built, and you already have tradesmen at your site.

What types of changes might arise in a remodeling project? Occasionally, a space that looks great on paper feels different when you walk through it at the framing stage. Perhaps it's a pantry that seemed sufficient on paper but feels too small once you see it in person. Conversely, you might realize that the extra wide hallway you thought you wanted is stealing too much space from an adjacent linen closet. Of course, a qualified professional remodeler should be able to point out standards and best practices long before you get to the framing stage. However, just as in new construction, if you realize that a change should be made, it is much less costly and invasive to do so while the project is underway than after the fact.

Regardless of which changes you are considering, having the financial wherewithal to successfully handle them can be the difference between being happy with your project and wishing that you had done something differently. That's why it's essential that you have a contingency fund and that you don't max out your budget. As we discussed in depth in Chapter 7, just because a bank says you can afford a certain amount doesn't necessarily mean that you should spend it. Planning a project that's a little under your financial comfort level can help give you a buffer in case of an emergency.

That's Life!

Which leads us to our next unexpected occurrence – life! Sometimes, the unexpected things that happen during a remodeling or new construction project have absolutely nothing to do with the project itself, and yet they can have a major impact on it.

The life changes that we're talking about can be wonderful – the impending birth of a new baby, a marriage proposal on the horizon, a foster child coming into your family or more. Sometimes, the life changes can be unexpected, but not bad, such as when an older child moves back home temporarily after college or due to a job loss, or an elderly parent moving in. At other times, an unexpected change in your health or financial situation can dramatically change the shape of your project.

That's why it's critical to be flexible as your project progresses. If you suddenly require more square footage, or if the room that you are adding needs to be made accessible, or if your project needs to be downsized due to an unexpected "hidden condition," that's when you have to be completely upfront and honest with your contractor. Don't try to hide the situation that you are dealing with, bring it front and center so that you can work together to find creative and constructive solutions to what initially appears to be problematic. Remember, an experienced professional contractor has most likely dealt with a similar circumstance before. They can offer creative solutions that will minimize the impact on your budget and give you a home that you'll still love.

Ultimately, open communication and proactive planning are your keys to a successful project – no matter what the challenge you are facing. We hope that this book has helped you recognize some common regrets and avoid them in your construction project, so that you and your family can enjoy it for many years to come.

About The Authors

Gary R. Palmer

Gary Palmer, a Licensed North Carolina Residential General Contractor and South Carolina Residential Builder, founded and remains President and Co-Owner of Palmer Custom Builders®' parent corporation since 1986, initially specializing in flooring, renovations and repairs. He holds a BS in Recreation Resources Administration with emphasis on National Resources Management from NC State University and an associate degree from Paul Smith's College, School of Forestry.

From those early roots to the wide diversity of projects that Palmer Custom Builders® routinely tackles today, Gary brings over 35 years of experience in remodeling, additions, custom homes, renovations and repairs. He provides clients with expertise in all phases of the construction process, including project management, estimating and sales, as well as creative design, construction solutions, engineering, site development, heavy equipment operations and landscaping. Thanks to his diverse experience, Palmer Custom Builders® is a Residential Design-Build firm today, working with clients from project conception to completion or collaborating with clients' architects or design firms as their needs require. In either case, clients benefit from Gary's passion and commitment to every project, diversified experienced and hands-on project management, ensuring that high standards of quality and fine workmanship are maintained, and timely progress is made on every project.

Yet it's Gary's desire to fulfill the unique needs of each client that comes through in everything his team does. "When we start a project, the entire team looks at it as if it were their own," Gary emphasizes.

Pam A. Palmer

Pam Palmer has more than 35 years of experience in management, advertising, sales, marketing, and general business practices and is also a licensed North Carolina Real Estate Broker. As Chief Financial Officer and Chief Operating Officer of Palmer Custom Builders® since 1996, Pam's common-sense approach ensures that the business operations and financial soundness of this well-established company remain on a solid footing. "Clients always value the reassurance that comes from dealing with a firm with our longevity and fiscal stability," she notes.

Pam oversees Palmer Custom Builders®' sales, design, operations and digital marketing endeavors. Her steady reassurance keeps operations running smoothly and ensures that the lines of client communication always remain open.

Trish Stukbauer

Trish Stukbauer is editor of *Re: Over Yonder* magazine and a former newspaper editor. She is Director of Communications for Holy Comforter Church in Charlotte, NC, and owns a marketing company, ie marketing, whose clients range from an international business incubator to a globally recognized home décor retailer as well as advertising agencies on both coasts and several authors and celebrities.

She is thrilled to have worked with Gary and Pam and called them friends for more than a decade. She began covering their projects for

Today's Custom Home magazine and then moved on to writing for their websites and social media.

"What really sets the Palmers apart is how they genuinely care for each client and treat every single project as if it was their own. There's a level of caring, competence and good old-fashioned integrity that you rarely see in business today that the Palmers and all their team members share that makes them unique."

CPSIA information can be obtained
at www.ICGtesting.com
Printed in the USA
BVHW040925130220
572217BV00004B/11